History

for 6–12 year olds
Transmissions and Res[ources]

SCHOOLS

Living Proof, How We Used to Live The Spanish Armada, Britons at War, From Iron Ways..., ...To Victorian Days, **Chuck Wallace's Middle Age Spread, Lisa Looks Back, Victorian Scots, Newes of the Weeke, Robert Burns: Alive and Kicking**

AGE 7–11

Living Proof

AUTUMN TERM 1998
Thursdays 9.40–10.00
SUBTITLES

1　**Britain in the Second World War**
　24 Sep 7977182

2　**Victorian Britain**
　1 Oct 7247642

3　**Life in Tudor Times**
　8 Oct 7083446

4　**Anglo-Saxons and Vikings in Britain**
　15 Oct 7812950

5　**Roman Britain**
　22 Oct 7658754

resources

Teachers' Guide
Includes ★ quiz sheets to complement the programmes ★ background information for teachers ★ suggestions for investigating the local history of your own area ★ photocopiable activity sheets. **£3.95**

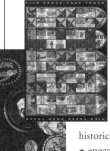

Activity Pack
Local History
Contains
★ teachers' booklet
★ full-colour A3 posters showing houses from four different historical periods
★ engaging full-colour timeline ★ colourful board game about the lives of rich and poor through history
★ 22 photocopiable activity sheets
★ 10 black-and-white A4 photocards.
Published by Channel Four Learning and Hodder and Stoughton. **£19.95**
(special offer)

Teachers' Book
Using Local History Sources
A valuable guide to locating and using various kinds of sources. Published by Hodder and Stoughton. **£13.99**

CD-ROM/CD-I
Living Proof
This interactive quiz game allows the player to select from over

100 film sequences, arranged by the periods and subjects of the programmes. Includes quiz questions and explanations of the answers with relevant historical details. CD-ROM for Acorn or PC. **£19.99***

Each additional CD-ROM (only with initial order) **£5.88***

Video
5 x 20-minute programmes. **£19.98***

HOW WE USED TO LIVE

AGE 7–11

The Spanish Armada

AUTUMN TERM 1998
Tuesdays 10.25–10.45
SUBTITLES

1　**The Spanish are coming**　drama
　3 Nov 3566135

2　**Family against family**　drama
　10 Nov 3239039

3　**Victory**　drama
　17 Nov 3068543

resources

Teachers' Guide
Provides background information and a range of activities for pupils.
£3.95

Resource Pack
Includes ★ maps ★ ships' lists
★ decision-making activities ★ notes for teachers. **£14.95**

Poster
The Spanish Armada
70 x 100 cm. Published by PCET.
£8.95*

Video
3 x 20-minute programmes.
£14.99*

Britons at War

AUTUMN TERM 1998
Tuesdays 10.25–10.45

1 **The Road to War** documentary
   22 Sep 9900613

2 **Nelson's Eye** drama
   29 Sep 9746417

3 **Run Rabbit, Run** drama
   6 Oct 7532983

4 **The Admiralty Regrets**
   documentary
   13 Oct 7378787

5 **Never Again** documentary
   20 Oct 7034391

resources

Teachers' Guide
Includes background information and activities for pupils based on historical evidence such as ration books and maps. **£3.95**

Resource Pack
Replica suitcase containing
★ 48-page booklet
★ notes for teachers
★ photocopiable activity sheets ★ four full-colour

reproductions of contemporary posters
★ full-colour timeline for the classroom wall covering the period 1930–1953
★ reproduction of a Second World War board game called 'Beat the Blitz'. **£19.99**

Video
5 x 20-minute programmes. **£17.99***

From Iron Ways...

SPRING TERM 1999
Tuesdays 10.25–10.45

1 **The Iron Cradle** documentary
   12 Jan 9595783

2 **Geordie Lads and Cornishmen** drama
   19 Jan 9331567

3 **Horses on the Wagon Way** drama
   26 Jan 9097171

4 **The Quaker Railway** drama
   2 Feb 9440821

5 **Great Britons and Local Heroes** documentary
   9 Feb 9286625

resources

Teachers' Guide
A wealth of ideas, resources and cross-curricular themes for children to explore. **£3.95**

Pupils' Book
Iron Ways
Discover how railways changed Britain. Illustrated throughout with contemporary paintings and photographs. Hardback. **£9.95**

Poster
Victorian Railways
Shows how rich and poor alike felt the effects as railway lines linked factory towns, villages, cities and seaside resorts. Published by PCET. 70 x 100 cm. **£8.95***

Video
5 x 20-minute programmes. **£35.25***

...To Victorian Days

SPRING TERM 1999
Tuesdays 10.25–10.45

1 **1845: A Time of Change** documentary
   23 Feb 9788033

2 **Family Cares** drama
   2 Mar 9357043

3 **Proper Jobs** drama
   9 Mar 9193847

4 **Fatal Mixture** drama
   16 Mar 9922351

5 **Rights and Wrongs** drama
   23 Mar 9695255

resources

Teachers' Guide
Includes ★ many photocopiable activities
★ searching maps for clues to the past
★ following a history trail ★ spinning and weaving ★ becoming a history detective
★ building a railway line. **£3.95**

Video
5 x 20-minute programmes. **£35.25***

Chuck Wallace's Middle Age Spread

SUMMER TERM 1999
Tuesdays 10.10–10.25

1 **The Ragman's Roll**
20 Apr 1369778

2 **The First Rising**
27 Apr 1198282

3 **Church and Crown**
11 May 8141343

4 **Bannockburn**
18 May 8987147

5 **Towards the Renaissance**
25 May 8716651

resources

Teachers' Guide £3.95

Video
5 x 15-minute
programmes. £14.99*

Lisa Looks Back

SUMMER TERM 1999
Thursdays 11.10–11.25

1 **Going to Granny's**
22 Apr 6195025

2 **Fun and Games**
29 Apr 6931829

3 **O'Donnell's Farm**
13 May 8005961

4 **Are We Nearly There?**
20 May 8778865

5 **Back to School**
27 May 8514669

resources

Teachers' Guide £3.95

Pupils' Book
Includes full-colour
information sheets and
activity sheets, drawing on
local experience and evidence
to explore life in the 1940s,
1950s and 1960s.
Published by Blackstaff Press. £4.99

Video
5 x 15-minute programmes. £14.99*

History for 6–12 year olds

order form

NAME

NAME AND ADDRESS OF SCHOOL

POSTCODE:

TELEPHONE:

ACCOUNT NUMBER IF KNOWN

Credit Card Details

Cross one: ☐ Visa ☐ Mastercard ☐ Delta ☐ Switch

Card number:

Valid from: (Month Year)   Expiry date: (Month Year)

Issue number (Switch):   Amount of payment: (£ pence)

Cardholder's Name (as on card):
Postal Address:

Postcode:

I authorise Channel 4 Schools to charge my account with the total amount of my
order. Orders will be fulfilled where possible according to the availability dates stated
in this order form. Availability dates refer to 1998 except where otherwise stated.

Cardholder's signature:

	AVAILABILITY	IPC	PRICE	QUANTITY	TOTAL
LIVING PROOF					
Living Proof Teachers' Guide	Aug	187778	£3.95		
Local History Activity Pack	Aug	217979	£19.95		
Using Local History Sources Teachers' Book	Aug	220200	£13.99		
Living Proof CD-ROM (PC)	Aug	145901	£19.99*		
additional CD-ROMs (PC)	Aug	199356	£5.88* each		
Living Proof CD-ROM (Acorn)	Aug	145849	£19.99*		
additional CD-ROMs (Acorn)	Aug	200494	£5.88* each		
Living Proof CD-I	Aug	145857	£19.99*		
additional CD-Is	Aug	200758	£5.88* each		
Living Proof Video	Aug	187066	£19.98*		

All prices marked * include VAT

	AVAILABILITY	IPC	PRICE	QUANTITY	TOTAL
THE SPANISH ARMADA					
The Spanish Armada Teachers' Guide	Aug	216928	£3.95		
The Spanish Armada Resource Pack	Dec	216959	£14.95		
The Spanish Armada Poster	Nov	220576	£8.95*		
The Spanish Armada Video	Dec	217389	£14.99*		
BRITONS AT WAR					
Britons at War Teachers' Guide	Aug	187777	£3.95		
Britons at War Resource Pack	Aug	164443	£19.99		
Britons at War Video	Aug	221502	£17.99*		
FROM IRON WAYS...					
From Iron Ways... Teachers' Guide	Aug	145294	£3.95		
Iron Ways Pupils' Hardback Book	Aug	146381	£9.95		
Victorian Railways Poster	Aug	217977	£8.95*		
Iron Ways Video	Aug	129274	£35.25*		
...TO VICTORIAN DAYS					
...To Victorian Days Teachers' Guide	Aug	145934	£3.95		
Victorian Days Video	Aug	145841	£35.25*		
CHUCK WALLACE'S MIDDLE AGE SPREAD					
Chuck Wallace Teachers' Guide	Aug	175956	£3.95		
Chuck Wallace Video	Aug	220249	£14.99*		
LISA LOOKS BACK					
Lisa Looks Back Teachers' Guide	Aug	177969	£3.95		
Lisa Looks Back Pupils' Book	Aug	220202	£4.99		
Lisa Looks Back Video	Aug	219569	£14.99*		
VICTORIAN SCOTS					
Victorian Scots Teachers' Guide	Dec	217388	£3.95		
Victorian Scots Video	Mar 99	217978	£14.99*		
NEWES OF THE WEEKE					
Teachers' Guide	Aug	167713	£3.95		
Video	Aug	191148	£14.99*		
ROBERT BURNS: ALIVE AND KICKING					
Robert Burns Teachers' Guide	Aug	164451	£3.95		
Robert Burns Video	Aug	177059	£14.99*		
All prices marked * include VAT				Total	

Channel 4 Schools
PO Box 100
Warwick
CV34 6TZ

Tel 01926 436444
Fax 01926 436446

Email sales@schools.channel4.co.uk

Please send a cheque made payable to Channel 4 Schools.
Postage and packing are **free**.

AGE 10–12

Victorian Scots

SPRING TERM 1999
Mondays 10.15–10.30

1 **Alexander Graham Bell**
11 Jan 9515527

2 **John Muir**
18 Jan 9344031

3 **Elsie Inglis**
25 Jan 9180835

4 **Andrew Carnegie**
1 Feb 9493913

5 **David Livingstone**
8 Feb 9239717

 resources

Teachers' Guide
Contains ★ background information for teachers ★ ideas for classroom discussion based around the programmes ★ activities to engage children's interest in Victorian Scotland. **£3.95**

Video
5 x 15-minute programmes. **£14.99***

AGE 7–11

Newes of the Weeke
Life in Stuart Wales

SUMMER TERM 1999
Fridays 10.25–10.40

1 **1631**
23 Apr 1295149

2 **1642**
30 Apr 1024653

3 **1648**
14 May 8077714

4 **1660**
21 May 8813518

5 **1674**
28 May 8642022

 resources

Teachers' Guide **£3.95**

Video
5 x 15-minute programmes. **£14.99***

AGE 10–12

Robert Burns:
Alive and Kicking

AUTUMN TERM 1998
● Night-time Wednesday 21 Oct 04.00–05.15 5037583
◗ SUBTITLES

1 **Mice and Lice**

2 **Amang Ye Takin' Notes**

3 **A Melodic Din to the Lugs**

4 **Warlocks in the Mirk**

5 **The Cauld Blast**

 resources

Teachers' Guide **£3.95**

Video
5 x 15-minute programmes. **£14.99***

4

Introduction

Welcome to this new vivid three-part drama which illustrates the fears and passions of the Elizabethan era: the fragility of peace, the danger of disunity and the confusion of religion and politics. The action is split between events in the English Channel and in rural Devon at the time of the Spanish Armada in 1588.

This guide provides a wealth of ideas and stimuli for developing an exciting child-centred, history-based topic around the Spanish Armada with many cross-curricular opportunities, including links between language skills and history.

Additional support is available through a poster focusing on the Spanish Armada and a resource pack containing maps, ships' lists, decision-making activities and teachers' notes for a journey to the Indies.

We hope you enjoy the programmes. Please send any comments, suggestions or examples of children's work to the address below. They are always most welcome.

Rick Hayes
Education Officer
Channel 4 Schools
PO Box 100
Warwick
CV34 6TZ

Using the programmes

Drama has a special place in the teaching of history. It offers a vivid picture of a past time that can be tested against other available evidence. This unit of three programmes tells the story of one of the most significant events of the Tudor period and tells it in a way that is both relevant and exciting while meeting the demands of the various curriculum requirements within the United Kingdom.

The programmes are a rich source of information that is both lively and accessible, but they are not designed to be used in isolation. By comparing this version of the facts with that in textbooks, historical fiction, pictures and records, children can begin to understand why interpretations of the past may differ.

Careful preparation ensures you get the most out of your viewing. Try to make time to:

▶ Read through the programme notes and familiarise yourself with the background information.

▶ Collect information books and pictures about Tudor times in general and the Spanish Armada in particular.

▶ Find out as much as you can about Tudor times in your own locality.

Teachers' Guide

This is designed to support your planning. It provides resources and ideas for preparation and follow-up but, as its name suggests, it is a guide, not a blueprint and it should be modified to meet the needs of your particular class.

The background points offer you, as a teacher, information on historical events and developments which you may wish to discuss with the class.

Before viewing

It is important that children take an active part in viewing and one way to develop an enquiring approach is by briefing your class, before each programme to look out for one particular theme or issue. Older children may wish to make brief notes on the chosen theme as they watch.

Key vocabulary

This section alerts you to any unfamiliar words that you may wish to introduce before the programme begins.

While viewing

The use of a freeze-frame, or pause facility, is not recommended on the first showing of the programmes to pupils. However, such techniques are useful when re-viewing. Well-chosen clips can be used to look at period details, to draw pupils' attention to particular events and to consider decisive moments at key points in the dramas.

Recap and consolidation

This enables you to check on literal recall and to unravel some of the more complex issues which are alluded to during the programmes. This can take the form of question and answer or discussion.

History provides an excellent context for developing the skills of literacy. On page 23 you will find ideas for using the series in this way, together with a book list of historical fiction set in the time of the Armada. In each programme one of the follow-up activities is flagged as **Literacy link**. These can be used to consolidate work covered as part of the Literacy Strategy in England.

Activities are backed up by differentiated worksheets to support independent investigation. The first sheet for each programme is designed for the younger or less able pupil, while the second sheet is aimed at those who are ready for a greater challenge.

Further suggestions for differentiation are included in the programme notes in order to meet the needs of pupils across the ability range.

Before watching the series with the class, it is suggested that you read the background information and then draw up a grid showing what you would expect pupils of differing abilities to know and understand by the end of the series.

Armed with this information you can set precise learning targets for groups or individuals within your class.

Cross-curricular links

Programmes	Content	Cross-curricular links in the Teachers' Guide
1. First Encounter	The coming of the Armada	The Armada story – Hi Spanish spies – Hi, En The road to war – Hi
	Attitudes and beliefs	Protestants and Catholics – RE
	Sir Francis Drake	'Drake's Drum' – En
2. Family Against Family	The progress of the Armada	Planning the invasion – Gg, En
	Family life	Family portraits – Hi, Art Making an impression – Art Furs and fabrics – Science, CDT
	The Tudor household	Tudor houses – Hi
3. Victory	The defeat of the Armada	The Armada story – Hi, En Viewpoints – Hi, En, PSE The Armada medal – Hi, CDT Shipwreck – Hi
	Attitudes and beliefs	Press conference – En, PSE
	Everyday life	Household objects – Science, CDT

Character list

Tom Byngham Aged 15; Protestant; son of a wealthy merchant; lives in Devon; apprentice to Francis Drake; hates Spain and Catholicism like his father but was previously betrothed to Anne Farley, a Catholic girl.

Anne Farley Aged 15; daughter of Catholic landowner; previously betrothed to Tom; at the time of the Armada is isolated, more than ever, by her religion; the servant, Jane, is the only friend she can really trust.

Jane Williams Aged 12; daughter of a fisherman killed at sea; servant to the Farley family; Protestant, though not devout; works hard to help her mother, Mary, support the family; criticised for working for a Catholic family.

Richard Byngham Aged 35; High Sheriff and commander of the militia; Protestant and anti-Catholic; emotional and passionate about his beliefs; loved and respected by his son, Tom.

Matthew Farley Aged 40; fervent Catholic; has been persecuted for his faith but remains strong; has been fined regularly by Byngham for not attending the Protestant church; proud to be English, he will not move abroad.

Lieutenant Bermudo Aged 25; professional soldier; brought up at the Spanish Court; son of an aristocrat; patriotic and a committed Catholic; carries orders from King Philip of Spain; resourceful, intelligent and ruthless.

Luis West African, originally taken as a slave by the Spanish; captured at the siege of Cartegena and since then a member of Drake's crew; bilingual; gentle and intelligent; forms a strong friendship with Tom.

1 First Encounter

Aims

This opening drama looks at the coming of the Armada and what it meant to the Elizabethans. It explores the beliefs and lifestyle of people of the period and looks at the divided loyalties of English Catholics at the time of the Armada.

Programme outline

It is 1588 and the Armada has been sighted off the coast of Cornwall. The warning beacons are lit and the English fleet sets sail from Plymouth to shadow the Armada up the Channel. One Spanish ship, the *Rosario*, falls behind and is captured by Sir Francis Drake. It is carrying a spy, Lieutenant Bermudo, who is hoping to make contact with English Catholics who may support the Spanish invasion force. Drake decides to hand Bermudo over to the High Sheriff, Sir Richard Byngham. Sir Richard's son, Tom, who is serving with Drake, is chosen to escort the prisoner along with Knox and Luis.

Meanwhile, on land, Sir Richard Byngham, a staunch Protestant, confronts his former friend, Matthew Farley. Once there were plans to marry Tom to Farley's daughter, Anne, but the Farleys have remained Catholics and, despite fines and threats of punishment, they have refused to convert. The betrothal was broken long ago and now, as the threat of invasion grows, Byngham has come to place Farley and his daughter under house arrest as potential traitors. Bermudo escapes on his way to Plymouth for interrogation. He has learnt that Farley is a Catholic sympathiser and he makes his way to the Farleys' house.

Background points

Throughout the 1580s, relationships between Spain and England were growing steadily worse. Religion, politics and economics all contributed to the tension.

- Spain was a Catholic country. England was Protestant. Philip II, the King of Spain, believed he had a divine mission to bring England back to the true faith.

- Spain was outraged when, in 1587, Elizabeth I of England executed the Catholic Mary Queen of Scots.

- When Philip's Protestant subjects in the Netherlands rebelled, England supported them.

- English sailors, such as Hawkins and Drake, attacked the Spanish treasure fleet as it brought silver from the New World back to Spain. They called it privateering. The King of Spain called it piracy. When Drake attacked Cadiz in 1587 and 'singed the king of Spain's beard' it was the last straw. Philip II gave orders to prepare for the invasion of Britain.

Before viewing

▶ Set the programme in time. Discuss other events and personalities from the Tudor period and place them on a time line. (See **activity sheet 12 on page 22**.)

▶ Talk about religious differences in Tudor times, including Henry VIII's break with Rome and Mary Tudor's return to Catholicism.

▶ Brief the children to look out for:

- Preparations for the Armada

- Different viewpoints about religion

- Problems faced by Catholics at the time

Key words

Catholic, Protestant, fleet, garrison, ransom, house arrest, beacon

After viewing

Recap and consolidation

▶ Drake had been ordered to proceed, showing a light to help other ships in the fleet stay in formation. He disobeyed those orders in order to capture a Spanish treasure ship. Was he right to do so?

▶ Why might English Catholics, like the Farleys, suffer from divided loyalties?

▶ What does the secret message say?

Spanish spies (activity sheet 1)

This is a good activity for developing reference skills. In addition to drawing information from the programme, children should be encouraged to use a small selection of topic books and to make notes as they go along. Teachers could ask children working in groups to research one theme and hot seat a representative from each group using questions like these:

- Will the English Catholics support the invasion?

- How are they getting ready for the Armada?

- How do people feel about their Queen?

Literacy link: collecting and presenting information from a variety of sources.

The road to war (activity sheet 2)

Encourage older and abler pupils to look for links between the different causes and to decide which they think are the most important.

Protestants and Catholics

Religious differences are central to the story of the Armada and children need to understand them in order to make sense of what happens in the drama. But these are living issues that must be handled with sensitivity. Characters in the drama were intolerant of the religious beliefs of others. Are we more tolerant today with regard to those who have different beliefs? Parallels can be drawn with issues in other parts of the world, in particular with those in Northern Ireland. If possible, invite representatives of each faith into the classroom to talk about the way they worship, or arrange a visit to a Catholic and Protestant church to compare the different styles.

Tudor churches

In most towns there is at least one parish church that was in use in Tudor times. Often it still holds clues to its past. Look for tablets and wall plaques dating from the 1500s. A list of vicars may give the name of the incumbent in the Armada year. Look at old furnishings, such as the font and porch door, and link these with the household furniture seen in the programme. Try to work out which parts were standing when Elizabeth was on the throne and which were added later.

'Drake's Drum'

The poem by Sir Henry Newbolt (**activity sheet 7**) presents Drake as a legendary hero. It's an exciting poem that works well as a choral speaking exercise and makes a good starting-point for an investigation of Drake himself. Was he really a hero? The English certainly thought so, but the Spanish saw him as a pirate and a thief and in the programme we see him deserting his post in order to capture a prize ship.

Children could look at some of the events in his life and use them to arrive at a judgement.

1540 Born near Tavistock in Devon

1567 Sailed to West Africa with Sir John Hawkins on a slaving expedition

1577 Attacked Spanish treasure ships in a journey that took his ships round the world

1581 Was knighted on his return to England

1587 Sacked Cadiz and captured Spanish treasure ships

1588 Played an important role in defeating the Spanish Armada

1590 Became a Member of Parliament for Plymouth and worked to provide the town with a good water supply

1596 Died of dysentery in the West Indies on his final voyage

---

Literacy link: Drake is a popular figure in historical fiction and he plays a part in several stories aimed at younger readers (see page 23). Try comparing the version presented in the drama with that in other sources.

Spanish spies

You are a Spanish spy. You are to go to Britain, spy out the land and then report back to His Majesty King Philip II of Spain. He wants you to find out about:

Religion in Great Britain

British defences against the Armada

The Queen and her courtiers

Whether English Catholics will support the invasion.

The road to war

Here are some important things that happened in Tudor times.

▶ Cut them out and make them into a time line.

Elizabeth I orders the execution of
Mary Queen of Scots (1587)

Sir Francis Drake attacks Spanish ships
and steals their treasure (1577 onwards)

Elizabeth is crowned Queen of
England and Wales (1558)

Sir Walter Raleigh returns from America
with tobacco and potatoes (1585–7)

William Shakespeare is born (1564)

The *Mary Rose* sinks (1545)

King Philip sends the Spanish Armada
(1588)

Henry VII defeats Richard III at
Bosworth Field (1485)

Some of these happenings caused Spain to become an enemy of England. Which are they and
can you explain why they made the Spanish angry?

2 | Family Against Family

Aims

This, the second programme, describes what happened when the Armada arrived, and examines its impact on men and women at different levels of Tudor society.

Programme outline

The Armada has reached the English Channel and is followed by the British fleet as it attempts to meet up with the Spanish army of invasion that is gathered in the Netherlands. Bermudo, the escaped Spanish spy, has reached the house of Matthew Farley. He wants Farley to help him to make contact with Catholic sympathisers who will raise an army to support the invasion.

But Farley refuses; his first duty is to his own country. The argument is interrupted by the arrival of Sir Richard Byngham and his militia to search the house. Anne hides the spy in a priest hole, and smuggles him out when the guards' backs are turned, but he wants more. He takes her hostage and orders her to find him a place of concealment until morning when he can get to Southampton to contact his friends.

Tom Byngham, who still has a fondness for Anne, goes along with Knox, Luis and the militiamen in search of Bermudo and, with the help of Anne's servant, Jane, succeeds in recapturing him. Bermudo claims that Matthew Farley willingly agreed to help him and Farley is arrested as a traitor. Tom Byngham knows he is innocent. Anne's servant, Jane, told him the whole story. But Tom is not there to defend Farley. He has returned to his ship and Farley faces the gallows.

Background points

The Spanish invasion was to be a two-pronged attack. The enormous Spanish fleet of 130 ships, 7,000 sailors and 17,000 soldiers was to sail down the Channel and link up with an army of occupation which had been mustered in the Netherlands. The purpose of the fleet was to destroy the British Navy and to ferry the invasion force across the Channel to Britain. Once landed in Kent, the army was to march on London.

The Spanish believed that they could rely on many sympathisers who would rally to their cause once the army had landed. These, they hoped, might include followers of the old faith, like the Farley household, and people disgusted by the execution of Mary Queen of Scots.

Before viewing

▶ On a map, trace the progress of the Spanish Armada along the English Channel, using the information below.

▶ Bermudo is planning to take a boat from Dartmouth to Southampton. Use the map to follow his journey.

▶ Brief the children to look out for:

● Details of costume and differences between the appearance of rich and poor

● Details of the furniture in Matthew Farley's house

● Different opinions about the Spanish invasion

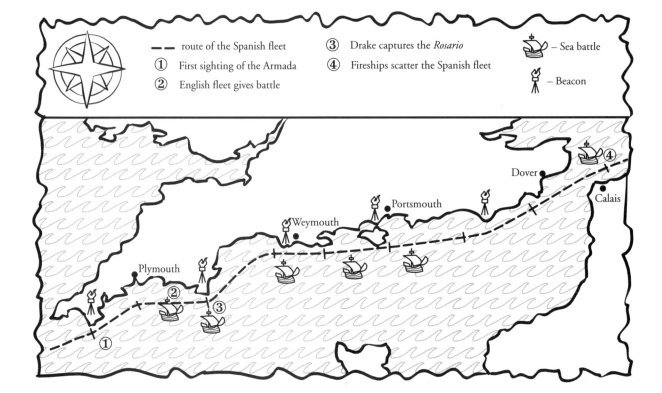

- - - route of the Spanish fleet
① First sighting of the Armada
② English fleet gives battle
③ Drake captures the *Rosario*
④ Fireships scatter the Spanish fleet
🚢 – Sea battle
🔥 – Beacon

Dover
Calais
Portsmouth
Weymouth
Plymouth

Key words

Priest hole, sanctuary, supply vessel, holy war, conspiring

After viewing

Recap and consolidation

▶ Why was Matthew Farley in such a difficult position? Was he a traitor or not? What do the children think?

▶ Why did Anne hide Bermudo? What else could she have done? Discuss with the children what they might have done in her place.

▶ Talk about some of the different attitudes to the Spanish expressed by characters in the drama.

Tudor houses (activity sheet 3)

▶ This is an extract from an inventory made after John Bussington's death. You can get an inventory for your own area from your local record office or from major public libraries. Allow time to decipher it yourself before trying it out on the children.

This one translates as follows:

In the hall
In primis (firstly) *a long broad and square board* (table)
Item ii benchis (benches), *ii stools and a chayre* (chair)
Item ii candelsticks and a spyce (spice) *crusher*
Item iii platters (large plates), *iiij porringers* (dishes for porridge) *and iii sawcers* (saucers)
Item iii salt spoons and a pewter cuppe.
Item i paire of tongs and fyer (fire) *pan.*
Item i curtin of yellowe vellet (velvet) *and his rod*

▶ Encourage children to look at more pictures or to research in reference books to find out what the interior of a Tudor house looked like. **Activity sheet 8** makes a good starting-point. Compare the picture presented in the drama with other evidence.

Operation invasion (activity sheet 4)

▶ This kind of problem-solving task helps children to understand the decisions taken by people in the past. The Spanish fleet set off in the summer, when the sea was calm. It sailed to La Coruna and across the Bay of Biscay before sighting the Cornish coast. The plan to pick up the Spanish Army in the Low Countries failed and so there was no opportunity to make the proposed landing in Kent.

▶ Use this, together with **activity sheet 1**, as part of a role-play in which groups of children take the part of Spanish generals and report back to King Philip about ideas for invading Britain. Older children could be asked to write a report in which they use all available evidence to put forward their case as persuasively as possible.

Literacy link: persuasive writing.

Family portraits

▶ **Activity sheet 8** shows a group portrait of a family of roughly similar status to those featuring in the drama. Encourage children to look carefully at the composition.

● Why is the family arranged in this particular way in the picture?

● Who are the most important people?

● What kind of family is it?

● What does the picture tell us about the family's beliefs?

● Why might it have been painted?

▶ Get groups of children to make a tableau of the picture. Ask each to take the role of one member of the family. Then ask them to speak, or write down their thoughts. What is their life like? How do they feel about other members of the family? What are their religious beliefs? How do they feel about the Spanish, about Sir Francis Drake, about Queen Elizabeth?

Making an impression

Compare the costumes worn in the programme with those shown in portraits of the time. Good quality postcard reproductions can be obtained from the National Portrait Gallery, St Martin's Place, London WC2H OHE (0171 306 0055 extension 223). The characters in the drama are, for the most part, wearing everyday clothes, whereas those in formal portraits of the time usually show their subjects in full court dress and present themselves in a way that gets across a particular image of their status and achievements. To get the point across, ask children to make up a portrait of a character from the drama. Remind them to think about the pose, the dress and symbols of status which they may wish to include in their picture.

Furs and fabrics

Talk about the fabrics used in the period and, if you can, provide a small handling collection of different materials, both natural and synthetic. Get children to sort out those which might have been used in Elizabethan times and those which are modern. Which is the best for keeping people warm? Which is most comfortable to wear? Which is the most waterproof? Brief the children on designing a fair test to find out the answer.

Tudor houses

In ye hall

In primis a long broad and square board
Item ii benchis, ii stools and a chayre
Item ii candelsticks and a spyce crusher
Item iii platters, iiij porringers and iii sawcers
Item iii salt spoons and a pewter cuppe
Item i paire of tongs and fyer pan.
Item 1 curtin of yellowe vellet and his rod

This is part of a list of furniture belonging to John Bussington of Wiltshire. It was made in 1588 – the year of the Armada. Some of the words are very old-fashioned, and some are spelt differently from the way we spell them today.

▶ Use the picture to help you work out what it says.

▶ Make a list of all the furniture in one of the rooms in Matthew Farley's house.

Operation invasion

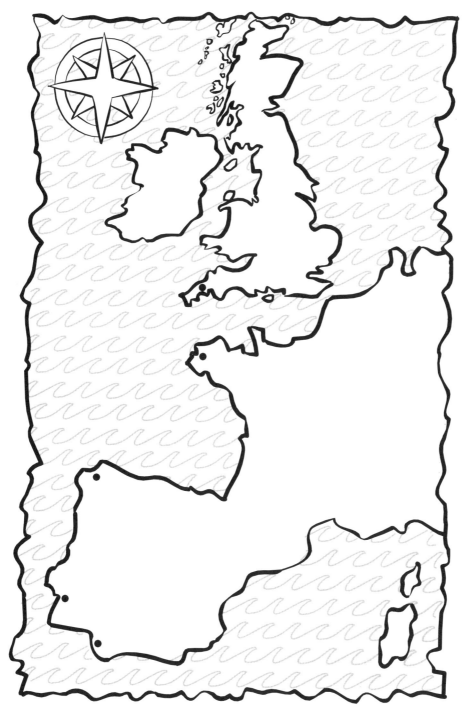

His Imperial Majesty, Philip of Spain commands you to plan the invasion of Britain.

▶ Decide on the best time of year for the invasion.

▶ Work out a route from Lisbon to the English Channel.

▶ Pick up the Spanish army which is waiting for you in the Low Countries.

▶ Decide on the best landing place on the British coast.

Write a letter back to His Imperial Majesty, explaining what you have done.

3 | Victory

Aims

This final programme looks at the departure of the Spanish Armada and examines its impact on people of the time, both on land and at sea.

Programme outline

The Armada has sailed up the English Channel and lies at anchor off Calais. The English commanders use fire-ships to scatter the fleet. It heads northward, pursued by the English navy.

Lieutenant Bermudo, mounted with wrists tied, is being prepared to leave for London, escorted by two mounted militiamen.

Matthew Farley is under house arrest accused of treason. Anne Farley slips out to Jane and her mother. Jane no longer dares to work for a Catholic family and urges Anne to change her religion.

Aboard the warship *Revenge*, Tom Byngham and Luis take part in a sea battle. Luis is killed and Tom is wounded.

The militiamen set fire to the cottage where Jane and her mother live, because Jane is associated with a Catholic family.

When Tom Byngham returns from sea, he confirms that Matthew is innocent of treason, but his father refuses to believe him, although Jane confirms his story. In a clash of wills, Tom dares to stand against his father and threatens to speak for Matthew Farley at his forthcoming trial. Byngham angrily backs down on this occasion, but there is no prospect of reconciliation with the Farleys and, as the programme ends, Anne sadly watches Tom ride away to a future without her.

Background points

The Spanish Armada succeeded in beating off the attacks of the English fleet as it sailed up the Channel, but problems arose when it attempted to link up with the invasion force in the Netherlands. The army was supposed to move up to Dunkirk for embarkation but when no word came from its leader, the Duke of Parma, the Armada took shelter in the harbour at Calais to await its arrival. The ships were closely packed and the appearance, in the middle of the night, of six fire-ships

packed with gunpowder, racing towards the Spanish fleet on the fast running tide, created an uncontrollable panic. Many of the captains simply cut their cables and fled. Those that held their station faced a ferocious English attack and a prevailing wind that drove them away from Calais and northwards towards Scotland. No attempt was made to return to the Channel. Instead the ships attempted to make their way back to Spain by rounding the north coast of Scotland and Ireland. Many were lost on the journey.

Before viewing

▶ On a map, trace the progress of the Spanish Armada along the English Channel.

▶ Brief the children to look out for:

● Details of life at sea including medical care for the wounded

● Household objects and what they are made of

● Reasons for converting from Catholicism to Protestantism

After viewing

Recap and consolidation

▶ Anne was tempted to give up her faith and become a Protestant. Talk about the decision with the children. What would they have done?

▶ Byngham thought that an English traitor deserved worse punishment than a Spanish spy. Why? What do the children think?

▶ Why was it so hard for Tom to defy his father? What does this tell us about relationships in Elizabethan times?

▶ Think of some examples, in all three programmes, of ways in which the characters' attitudes and reactions were different from those of today.

The Armada story (activity sheet 5)

This sheet can be used to consolidate the knowledge and understanding of younger or less able children. However, it also provides a good framework for a piece of extended narrative writing designed to test the older and more able pupils. In this case, after sequencing the different events, children should be asked to choose two more events, and add them to the sequence. They then expand on each caption, using the brief phrases as scaffolding for a longer piece of writing.

Literacy link: the development of the ability to organise writing in paragraphs.

Viewpoints (activity sheet 6)

A study of the Armada helps children to understand why the same event in history can be interpreted differently. There are clear, obvious conflicts between the Spanish and the English version of what happened. Go through the quotations with the group before asking children to decide which are Spanish and which English. You could allot one each to confident readers. Ask them to decide on the mood of the person who is speaking or writing and to show this in their reading.

The speakers are:

1. *Don Francisco de Bobadilla, a Spanish captain*

2. *Lord Howard, Admiral of the Fleet*

3. *Queen Elizabeth I*

4. *Spanish courtier*

5. *Richard Hakluyt, a contemporary chronicler*

6. *Sir Francis Drake*

7. *Inscription on a medal issued by the citizens of London to commemorate the victory*

8. *Two sailors on the* San Juan de Portugal *shipwrecked off the Irish coast*

Press conference

This drama exercise consolidates children's understanding of different points of view. Get some of the children to take the role of Spanish or English eyewitnesses. They might choose to be characters from the drama, or people quoted in **activity sheet 6, Viewpoints, page 15**. Other children take the role of reporters, gathering information for a story about the Armada for either an English or a Spanish paper. Hot seat the eyewitnesses to find out what actually happened, and how each feels about it. For example:

- 'Lord Howard, what's it like commanding Sir Francis Drake?'

- 'King Philip, do you feel in any way to blame for the disaster?'

- 'Captain, what were your thoughts as the ship crashed into the Irish coastline?'

Journalists should be encouraged to make brief notes which are written up into a full report using **activity sheet 9a** and **activity sheet 9b**.

Literacy link: taking notes, presenting a point of view.

Household objects

Talk about some of the artefacts seen in the programme. What were they made of? How were they made? Genuine Tudor artefacts are hard to get hold of, but you can assemble a small handling collection of vessels and get children to decide which were made of materials used in Tudor times.

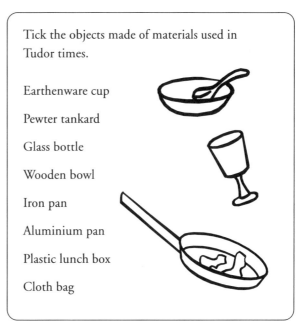

Tick the objects made of materials used in Tudor times.

Earthenware cup

Pewter tankard

Glass bottle

Wooden bowl

Iron pan

Aluminium pan

Plastic lunch box

Cloth bag

The Armada story

English fire ships scatter the Spanish fleet	Philip II of Spain decides to conquer England
Drake captures the *Rosario*	Spanish and English ships fight off the coast at Plymouth
Many Spanish ships are wrecked on their journey home	The Armada is sighted off the coast of Cornwall

Use both the television programme and reference books to help you to either:

▶ make an accurate drawing to go in each box

▶ write the story of the Armada using the boxes

Cut out the six boxes and place them in the correct order.

　　HOW WE USED TO LIVE　THE SPANISH ARMADA

Viewpoints

1 We found that many of the enemy (English) ships were better than ours in their design and in their guns, gunners and crews… so that they could do with us as they wished.

2 Their force is wonderful great and strong and yet we pluck their feathers by little and little.

3 I know I have the body of a weak and feeble woman, but I have the heart and stomach of a king, and of a king of England too.

4 His Majesty has felt it (the defeat of the Spanish Armada) more than you would believe possible. I do not know how he could bear such a blow.

5 The Queen's Majesty rode into London in triumph, to give thanks for (the country's) glorious deliverance.

6 We have time to finish the game and beat the Spaniards too.

7 God blew with his winds and they were scattered.

8 Out of this ship died four or five every day of hunger and thirst. There is left very little bread but what they brought out of Spain, which stinks marvellously. Those in the ship do say they will rather go into the ground themselves than come in such a journey again for England.

▶ Here are some things that were said, or written at the time of the Spanish Armada. See if you can work out which show:

● the Spanish point of view

● the English point of view

Drake's Drum

by Sir Henry Newbolt (1862–1938)

Drake he's in his hammock and a thousand miles away
(Captain art thou sleeping there below?)
Slung between the round shot in Nombre Dios Bay
And dreaming all the time of Plymouth Hoe
Yonder looms the Island, yonder lie the ships
With sailor lads a-dancing heel-and-toe
And the shore lights flashing, and the night tide dashing
He sees it all so plainly as he saw it long ago.

Drake he was a Devon man, and ruled the Devon seas
(Captain art thou sleeping there below?)
Roving though his death fell, he went with heart at ease
And dreaming all the time of Plymouth Hoe.
Take my drum to England, hang it by the shore
Strike it when your powder's running low
If the Dons sight Devon, I'll quit the port of Heaven
And drum them up the Channel as we drummed them long ago.

Drake he's in his hammock till the great Armadas come,
(Captain art thou sleeping there below?)
Slung between the round shot, listening for the drum
And dreaming all the time of Plymouth Hoe
Call him on the deep sea, call him up the Sound
Call him when you sail to meet the foe;
Where the old trade's plying and the old flag flying
They shall find him ware and waking, as they found him long ago.

(Sir Francis Drake was born in 1540 and died in 1596 during
a voyage to the West Indies. He was buried at sea. There is a
legend in Devon that his drum can still be heard beating
and that he will come back to save his country
when she is again in danger.)

Family portrait

This picture is called 'A Family Saying Grace before the Meal'. It was painted round about 1585 – three years before the Spanish Armada.

Look at it carefully. How much can you find out about the family?

History headlines (English version)

5 AUGUST 1588

THE TUDOR TIMES

VICTORY!

You are a journalist writing for an English paper at the time of the Armada. Write the story from the English viewpoint.

Remember to include a picture and an interview with Sir Francis Drake and other eyewitnesses.

History headlines (Spanish version)

5 AUGUST 1588

THE SPANISH SUN
Disaster!

You are a journalist writing for a Spanish newspaper at the time of the Armada. Write the story from a Spanish viewpoint.

You should include a picture and an interview with King Philip II of Spain and other eyewitnesses.

Shipwreck

Underwater archaeologists have explored this Spanish ship.

Here are some of the things they found.

See if you can work out what they are for.

(1) candlestick (2) wooden wine cup (3) pottery jug (4) leather bottle (5) jawbones of pig (6) shoe (7) cannon-balls and shot (8) cannon (9) hour glass (10) pottery bowl

The Armada medal

Design your own Armada medal.

A Tudor family tree

▶ Use the pictures and information books to help you to fill in the names on this Tudor family tree.
▶ Find out which members of the family were Catholic and which were Protestant.

History and the framework for literacy

It is recommended that, where appropriate, literacy teaching should be linked to work in other areas of the curriculum. This unit of programmes provides an excellent stimulus for work on texts during the Literacy hour and at other times of the day when children are practising the skills of information retrieval and research.

Work on fiction and poetry

There are several good historical novels and poems about the adventures of Sir Francis Drake. They include:

Sir Francis Drake; His Daring Deeds by Roy Gerrard (Gollancz) ISBN 0-575-0487-4. A lively, rhyming story suitable for 7–9 year olds.

Drake's Drummer Boy by Pauline Francis (Anglia Young Books) ISBN 0-871173-56-6. Tells the story of Drake's voyage round the world from the point of view of his young drummer boy. An exciting story, easy to read to 8+ year olds.

All the Gold in the World by Robert Leeson (A&C Black, Flashbacks) ISBN 0-7136-4059-6. A well-written, reflective story with a real sense of period. Sufficiently short and accessible to tempt the reluctant older reader (9+ years).

'Drake's Drum' by Sir Henry Newbolt (see activity sheet 7)

Children could use any of the above books to:

● Compare different stories about Sir Francis Drake (7–8 years)

● Understand how the historical setting often influences events, incidents and the behaviour of characters (8–9 years)

● Investigate the features of different fiction genres, including historical fiction and narrative poetry (9–10 years)

● Compare and evaluate the treatment of Sir Francis Drake in the TV programme **The Spanish Armada** and in one of the historical novels listed above (10–11 years)

Work on non-fiction

● Recognise the difference between factual books about Sir Francis Drake and fictional stories of the kind listed above (7–8 years)

● Begin to distinguish between facts and opinions in information books and historical novels about Sir Francis Drake (8–9 years)

● Evaluate texts by comparing how different sources, including the television drama, treat the same information about the Armada (9–10 years)

● Distinguish between fact, opinion and fiction, using a range of material from the Teachers' Guide and the television drama (10–11 years)

One excellent text resource, often overlooked is the new series of 'Horrible Histories' such as *The Terrible Tudors* by Terry Deary and Neil Tonge, ISBN 0-590-55290-2. It is one of several in the series which contains a version of the story of the Armada. These books are easy to get hold of and children enjoy them. Try comparing one with an information book for an entertaining analysis of style and presentation.

Places to visit

The North

The Maritime Museum, Albert Dock, Liverpool
(0151 207 0001)

Demonstrations of crafts including sail and rope
making and barrel making.

East Riddlesden Hall, Keighley, West Yorkshire
(01535 607075) Film location for the interiors
of Matthew Farley's House.

The South

The Mary Rose Museum, Royal Naval Base,
Portsmouth (01705 751520)

The remains of a mid-sixteenth-century warship and
the weapons, clothing and personal possessions of the
soldiers and seamen who drowned when she sank.

The Tudor Merchant's House, Bugle Street,
Southampton (01703 224216)

The Shipwreck Heritage Centre, Rock-a-Nore Road,
Hastings, East Sussex (01424 437452)

Buckland Abbey, Yelverton, Devon PL20 (01822
853607) This is Sir Francis Drake's house. It contains
a number of ship models, together with his drum.

Montacute House, Montacute, Somerset. A fine
Elizabethan house which contains an excellent
collection of Tudor portraits on loan from the National
Portrait Gallery.

London

The National Maritime Museum, Greenwich
(0181 858 4422) Ships' models, paintings, maps
and navigational equipment.

The *Golden Hind*, St Mary Overy Dock, Southwark
(0171 403 0123)

The National Portrait Gallery, St Martin's Place,
London WC2 0NE (0171 306 0055)

Scotland

The National Museum of Scotland, Chambers Street,
Edinburgh (0131 225 7534)

Wales

The Welsh Industrial and Maritime Museum, Cardiff
Bay, Cardiff, Wales (01222 481919)

General

For details of Elizabethan buildings in your area
contact:

The National Trust, Education Department
(0171 222 9251)

English Heritage Education Service, Keysign House,
429 Oxford Street, London, WIR 2HD
(0171 973 3000)